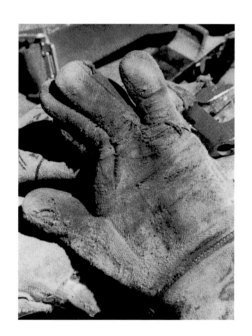

Iron

Iron:

ERECTING THE WALT DISNEY CONCERT HALL

GIL GARCETTI · FOREWORD BY FRANK O. GEHRY

BALCONY PRESS LOS ANGELES

Contents

Foreword

My first experience with ironworkers was in 1962. At that time, I was working on a small apartment building in Santa Monica. I couldn't believe how these men commanded the large pieces of iron flying through space. I thought how thrilling the work must be for them, like playing with a giant erector set. Forty years later, despite innovations in technology and new approaches to design, the role of ironworkers has changed very little. Ironworkers still need agility, physical strength, and ingenuity to get their job done. Their work is essential to the overall structure.

As the Walt Disney Concert Hall nears completion, the structure erected by the ironworkers will all but disappear behind exterior panels of stainless steel and the interior finishes. The individuals responsible for creating it are a set of highly skilled men and women whose work requires both physical and mental stamina. In the face of personal risk and grueling schedules, the ironworkers' contribution to architecture and, on a grander scale, the development of cities, is admirable.

Rarely has high-quality steel fabrication and construction been so crucial as with the Walt Disney Concert Hall. Its unconventional geometric forms coupled with stringent earthquake regulations, made the ironworkers' task all the more difficult. It is hard to believe that the robust musculature you see coming to life on these pages evolved from something quite delicate—classical music.

The history of the building dates back over fifteen years to Lillian Disney, and her desire to honor her late husband's commitment to the arts with a gift to Los Angeles. She was seeking a project that could be appreciated by the entire city but that also had cultural value—the Music Center was a natural recipient. Moreover, Lillian knew her husband possessed a deep love and affection for classical music and she was convinced that Los Angeles needed a world-class concert hall. At that point, Ernest Fleischmann had spent many years building the reputation of the Los Angeles Philharmonic. Confident that the orchestra would someday be one of the world's top five, the building was conceived as a place to showcase the Philharmonic. In fact, the 1987 competition called not for a downtown tourist attraction but rather the world's greatest concert hall.

Because the focal point of the building is the concert hall itself, we essentially designed the structure from the inside to the outside. To ensure the primary function was satisfied, our office went through over 50 iterations and enlisted the participation of Esa-Pekka Salonen, the orchestra members, and acoustician Yasuhisa Toyota. In quest of a synthesis of acoustics and architecture, the solution was a room shaped like a box but with a sculptural seating arrangement. I likened it to the idea of a boat in a box; hence the evolution of the sailing metaphor. The ceiling started to be shaped like sails and then the outside started to be shaped like sails.

Typically, it is complicated to translate an internal vision to exterior surfaces, particularly when dealing with complex geometries. However, we were able to realize the design for the concert hall with CATIA, a three-

dimensional surface-modeling program developed for the aerospace industry. While it may have been possible to build without the program, the computational requirements alone would take decades. We have been working with this program for fifteen years and have become increasingly reliant on its technology, which allows us to digitize our wood and paper models to generate a continuously curved surface model and series of surface points. Nevertheless, we really pushed the envelope on the concert hall.

The CATIA model served as the primary source of information. Conventionally, each trade starts with a blank sheet of paper. The architect has drawings, the structural engineer has another set of drawings, and the steel detailer has yet another set of drawings. However, with the CATIA

"I think Gehry is the ironworkers' hero. Every ironworker likes a good challenge and Frank Gehry throws an awfully good challenge."
—Johnny O'Kane

model, a collaborative process ensued. All the construction trades contributed to, and utilized, the CATIA model to execute their respective responsibilities. It also enabled the entire project team to track a virtual building just ahead of the actual one so problems were apparent before they occurred. For example M.A. Mortenson Company, the general contractor, operated a three-dimensional scheduling sequence that actually manufactured the steel in the same order the ironworkers assembled the building frame. Dealing with exact information and quantifiable linear feet of steel, the CATIA model encouraged efficient site planning and coordination.

CATIA also allowed extremely complicated steel to go together on the site without the kind of problems that happen on similar sized buildings. Due to the consistency of information and the precision of the calculations, every element tied back to an origin. When an ironworker was on the scaffolding, he could get someone to survey him a point and know he was within an eighth of an inch.

Despite the benefits CATIA brought to the project, the concert hall still provided a challenge for the ironworkers. Even the most seasoned ironworker has most likely never worked on a project quite this complex. If it is a box, they know what it is going to look like, but with the concert hall they didn't have a clue so they were wondering as they went

along. Due to the unusual forms, including box columns that lean 17 degrees, they had to be creative about rigging, scaffolding, and safety.

Charged with the grave responsibility of erecting a structure that can withstand the forces of nature, the role of the ironworkers is critical. Because of the atypical geometry, we've known from the beginning that the integrity of the concert hall was directly related to the steel. Subsequently, we reverse engineered it down to the steel. We knew if we got the steel right, we would get the building right. If we got it wrong, the concert hall would never be realized.

When the concert hall is finished, there will be two places where visitors can catch a small glimpse of the steel frame: through the skylight in the pre-concert room and in an exit stairway that heads into the garden between the pre-concert room and Founders' Room. In these fragmented and isolated forms, however, one has only a sense of the enormity of the entire configuration that lies beneath, above and around you.

The ironworkers have been extremely successful in carrying out my vision and what they have put in place is, in itself, a piece of art. Exploring the relationship between process and product in the case of the Walt Disney Concert Hall provides an interesting dichotomy. On the one hand, there is a structure composed of massive steel; but when you consider what is actually inside, it is very

refined and elegant. Both graceful in their own way, the music that eventually infiltrates the space and, although concealed, the framework that defines it, will form a lasting impression on the cultural landscape of the city.

Erection stories tend to be overlooked and it is my hope that this book will draw attention to the forgotten heroes of architecture. For them, ironwork is more than a job. It is a calling. Ironworkers know, and I know, that most people would never think twice about doing their work. The vast majority of the population will never realize the significance of their fundamental role in this project. I am delighted that Gil's book will honor the workers that make our designs a reality.

—FRANK O. GEHRY

Structure

T the wondrous geometry of the
Walt Disney Concert Hall stops
most people who see the iron
skeleton of the building. The swooping
sails of the south side together with
the massive S-shaped columns and 17-
degree, forward-leaning columns on
the north side are indeed impressive.
But that wonder pales next to the
experience of being within the dense
forest of iron underneath the columns
or of looking directly down 120 feet.

**The accompanying
photographs**
attempt to convey
the art and beauty
of the raw iron in its
various geometric
forms. There are
over 12,000 pieces
of iron, none identi-
cal to another.
Placed end-to-end
they would stretch
49 miles.

On the construction site on a late Saturday afternoon in January, an ironworker came up to me and said,

"Whoever had the vision for something like this must be a genius. It is interesting how few of us use much of our brain. Whoever dreamed this building certainly has, and he has made us use more of our brains."

Lucian Carlier, the foreman of a raising gang, was astounded with the iron he and his gang were asked to hang. Driving to the job site in the morning he was constantly amazed to see that it was still standing. "Cool, it's still there! Right on." he would say to himself.

"When you build something like this there is always a part of you that is a little uncertain until you actually see if it works. Then you say, 'Hey, that's pretty neat.'" says Trailer Martin, president, John A. Martin & Associates, structural engineers. Martin has been a structural engineer for 32 years. His company has been the structural engineers for many large projects including Staples Center and the Las Vegas Eiffel Tower. He has never worked on a project of this magnitude and complexity; "...nothing near as complicated as this. It's very exciting and we are very proud of our involvement."

"I first heard about this project ten years ago when American Bridge was going to do the iron. I told them I wanted to work on it. It was going to be an exciting job with multiple raising gangs. You hardly ever get the chance to work on a project with multiple raising gangs. Ten years later I was given the chance and I am very proud and excited. For so long I thought that the structure looked like a shipwreck, with iron pointing in all directions. But then you began to see all this iron shape the building. It's the most exciting building I've ever worked on. Too bad most people won't see the bones."
—Ernesto Penublas, ironworker
15 years, various gangs

"Some of these ribs can roll over on you in a flash. I've had them flip over on me out here. Because you don't know where its center of gravity is and it shifts as you raise it. You find it eventually but it spooks everyone out because you don't know what it's going to do."
—Lucian Carlier, 41, ironworker 24 years

Sophisticated three-dimensional modeling software made the complicated geometry possible. Terry Bell, architect and on-site project leader, said the project could have been built without it, but, including the seven or eight years the project had already taken, it would still require many more years of drawing before construction would start.

Acrobatics

"This is it! It's the whole thing, working together, building things; it's dangerous; it's an adrenalin rush; you're right there, you're living on the edge all day long. That's pretty cool."
–Doug Brastchi, 32, ironworker 3 1/2 years, bolt-up gang

"Hanging iron is what I do. I love the climbing and connecting part of the job. When I first started you could climb anywhere without a harness or being tied off. I was like a monkey. It was neat. The kick in the pants comes from the danger, the risk involved. Every piece of iron is different and if you don't treat each one as different it will whip you. The huge 17-degree leaning box columns were a kick. They didn't look right. We're used to hanging iron that is perfectly straight up and down. You have to get in there and be physical with the iron."
—Craig Castor, 36, raising gang

"We are very, very proud of what we accomplish and get through together. We are very strong as a brotherhood because we rely on each other so much, life and limb. That is what bonds and unifies us."
– Scotty Jackson, 31, raising gang

"My men (and one woman) are in the middle
of nowhere. They are 100-plus feet up without
anything below them. We've never had a job
like this."

—Jack Colin, ironworker 25 years, welding foreman

"The most sought after people on a construction site are the welders. It's a very high skill. The most important thing in the structure are the welds."
—Jim Glymph FAIA, architect and partner, Gehry Partners

"On this particular job you really have to watch your step. There are no floors; you are in mid-air; nothing is straight; everything is crooked; gravity is always against you. You really need to know where everyone around you is and they need to know where you are. This is an engineering feat. The building is just awesome."
—Thomas Pico Sr., 58, ironworker 25 years, production welding gang

Lance Harris is a "bolter-upper", coming in behind the "connectors" to securely attach the iron members with heavy bolts. A fourth generation ironworker and single parent of two he says, "I would be proud to have my son join me as an ironworker."

"With the work I've done here, nothing is impossible. If they can dream it up, we can do it."
—Mark Seymour, 39, ironworker for 21 years, raising gang

"You have L.A.'s finest ironworkers out here. If you couldn't cut it, you were gone. This was a unique job unlike any other I had worked in my 21 years as an ironworker. As the union steward my first priority is safety. Whatever it would take to get the job done safely, we do it. I don't care if it takes five hours to do a job that normally takes one hour. I've seen too many men killed or seriously injured."
—Brent May, ironworker 21 years, union steward

"Ironworkers earn their money."
–Trailer Martin, President,
John A. Martin & Associates,
structural engineers

"Unlike virtually any other job, every weld
on this job is inspected because each weld
is important to the stability of the building.
The welding has been extremely difficult
because the geometry of the building is
so difficult."
–Vernon Gong, project superintendent,
John A. Martin & Associates, structural
engineers

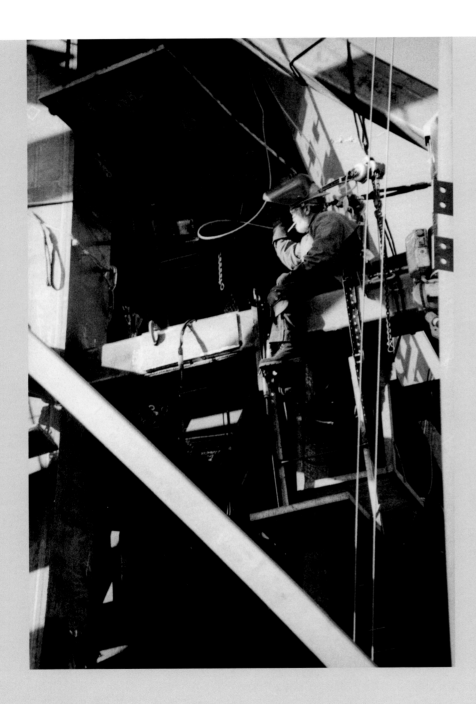

All welders need an occasional break.

When street passersby stare at the building they comment on the shapes and angles of the building and about the acrobatic work of the ironworkers. The density of iron is never mentioned. Bobby Casso, who has worked with iron for 28 years and is a job superintendent for Herrick, the project's structural iron supplier, has never seen as much concentrated iron as on this project. Twenty two million pounds of primary steel rest on the building's footprint.

"Everything we were taught—plumb, level, layouts—is thrown out the window with this project. You must think out of the box to get this job done. The structure is always moving because of the design, weight and weather. Our job as ironworker "finishers" is to carefully, and with an artist's touch, secure the stainless steel panels on the outside of the building. —Mitch Shanholtzer, project manager, Permasteelisa

Jose Para, 27, has been an ironworker for seven years working in the welding gang. He believes that the most challenging part of building the structure, for all ironworkers, has been the building's radical geometry. "Everything is at an axis or out of square. You don't know how the iron will react. You have to be especially careful about tools dropping and seriously injuring a fellow ironworker. And you have to watch out for your own safety."

"To be an ironworker you need to be kind of tough, kind of stubborn and semi-intelligent. Sometimes the brawn thing is not going to work and you're going to have to use your brain or you're going to get your butt kicked by the iron."

—Lucian Carlier, 41, ironworker 24 years

Raising

"Hanging iron," as the ironworkers refer to their work, begins at the construction site with the ground crew or "raising gang." The "hooker-uppers" have the responsibility of hooking the iron column or beam to the crane. This is critical work. If the iron is not attached properly, it can easily turn or shift as the crane begins to lift it; or, once high in the air it could begin to spin out of control. A properly hoisted piece of iron can save the connector hours of trying to work the iron into position.

Here a 70-foot long column wrapper is about to be hoisted to the top of the building.

Once the iron is overhead, the crane operator cannot see it. The solitary figure on
the roof of the building is the "phone
man." It is the "phone man" who directs
the crane operator where and how to place
the iron. Every ironworker respects the
importance of that job: responsibility for
the safety of his two connectors as well as
for any other workers who could be killed
or seriously injured if the iron column is
not properly controlled.

As soon as possible the iron is grabbed by one of the two connectors, who are both on an extension ladder approximately 110 feet off the ground. They eventually climb off the ladder to insert temporary bolts between the raised iron and a previously secured piece of iron. Later, other members of the raising crew, "bolter-uppers," will make the final attachment.

Bolting Up

Much of the work done by the "connectors" is done while straddling, kneeling
or standing on a beam. Working with their
"phone man" they carefully, but quickly,
move the beam into position.

These photos show
the two connectors
"working the iron."
They are manipulating
the iron beam into
place where they will
secure it with tempo-
rary bolts.

Workers

The ironworkers on the following pages are but a few of the nearly 200 who have helped build the Walt Disney Concert Hall. They come from different backgrounds but the one thing that unites them is their pride in the ironworker tradition. The other building trades cede leadership to the iron-workers as long as the ironworkers are on the job. For instance, on September 11 it was the ironworkers who shut down the concert hall construction site when they walked off the job in solemnity and tribute to the victims of the terrorist attacks. Their pride, in part, comes from the dan-gerous nature of the work they do and the knowledge that few people would do what they do everyday. Ironworker, Mark Seymour, a twenty one-year veteran, explained, "In our work we know we could be killed or seriously injured at any time and without warning. That means that the brothers you work with must be persons you trust – the brother working as your partner, the brother working over and below you. It is that trust you have in your brother ironworkers that helps build that pride."

Johnny O'Kane emigrated from Ireland with his mother and father when he was three years old. His father was an iron-worker in the old country, " . . . but I guess there were more bridges and buildings to build in America." At 22, twenty two years ago, Johnny became an ironworker. "Working together with my dad were some of the best days of my life. Holding a piece of iron between us were some of the greatest times we had." Johnny was a "phone man" with a raising gang. "It's a very stressful job. You have the lives of your partners in your hands as you tell the crane operator where to position the iron. I think Frank Gehry is an ironworker's hero. Every ironworker likes a good challenge and Frank Gehry throws an awfully good challenge."

Sue Egberts has been an ironworker for "15 wonderful years." She is one of eight women in a union membership of 2500. She is a welder who proudly says, "I pull my own weight. I carry my own stuff. This project has been so neat. It is so unique. The architecture, the weld joints were incredibly challenging. I am so proud to be part of this landmark."

"The grandest part of
being an ironworker is
being around that
crane. That's where the
building is being put
together. It's growing
and everyone else
comes behind."
—Lucian Carlier, raising
gang foreman

Richard Wagenen and
Allen Piney are "finish"
ironworkers. On this
job, finish workers are
responsible for attach-
ing the concert hall's
"curtain wall," the
stainless steel panels
that are the exterior
skin of the building.

I asked Johnny O'Kane to tell me about
the special pride that all ironworkers carry.
"For example, why do ironworkers have
more pride than carpenters?" I asked.
When he heard the question, Johnny's
head reacted as if I had slapped him. Then
he slowly leaned forward and looked me in
the eye. He said, "Gil, I used to be a reli-
gious man until I found out that Jesus was
a carpenter."

"My welding and the
design of the building
is what is going to keep
this building together
in an earthquake. I
want a challenge in my
work and this job sure
gave it to me."
—Joe Martinez Jr., 42,
ironworker 13 years,
welder

"There is absolute pride in being an ironworker. Pride comes in part because you
and others know how dangerous structural
iron work is and if you've done it for a
while that means your peers respect you
and your work."
—Darrel Cowles, 36, connector

Bill Deyling was a "phone man" with a "raising gang." He has been an ironworker for 32 years. His father was an ironworker and tried to keep Bill from becoming one. A friend helped him join the union. "It's a great feeling to walk away from the job and know that you and your 4 or 5 partners put up every stick of iron in the building."

This "welding detail gang" is holding some of
the tools they use "to work the iron" before
they can weld it. "There is nothing typical
about this job. We are constantly fighting
gravity because everything is laying out away
from you. This is the toughest job I've ever
had and I've worked on rigs in the ocean."
—Efren Tinoco, 53, weld detail gang foreman

Every weld is inspected and must pass ultrasound testing. Dave Lippencott, a weld inspector admired the work, "The union has given us their best. I rarely find an objectionable weld." Less than .01% of all welds have been rejected.

Joe Connery, 23, a connector with the
raising gang, respects the iron he works.
"You always have to be on top of it or
the iron will get you."

As an apprentice ironworker Cliff Neves
sets the floating scaffolds for the welders.
"Sometimes you are setting a float for the
welders and the beam begins to sway. It's
scary but it's also fun." Most ironworkers at
the job site could not recognize architect
Frank Gehry. When Neves met Gehry he told
him, "You made a crazy, fun building."

Tools

Around the waist of each member of the
raising gang is a collection of tools weighing nearly 60 pounds. The tools are used
to pull, bend, pry, force and work the iron
into position. When those tools can't do
the job, heavier tools like "come-a-longs"
and "turnbuckles" are used to work the
iron into position. Spud and crescent
wrenches were used to tighten the
530,000 pounds of nuts and bolts used in
hanging the iron. Many ironworkers go
through a new pair of gloves every two to
three days.

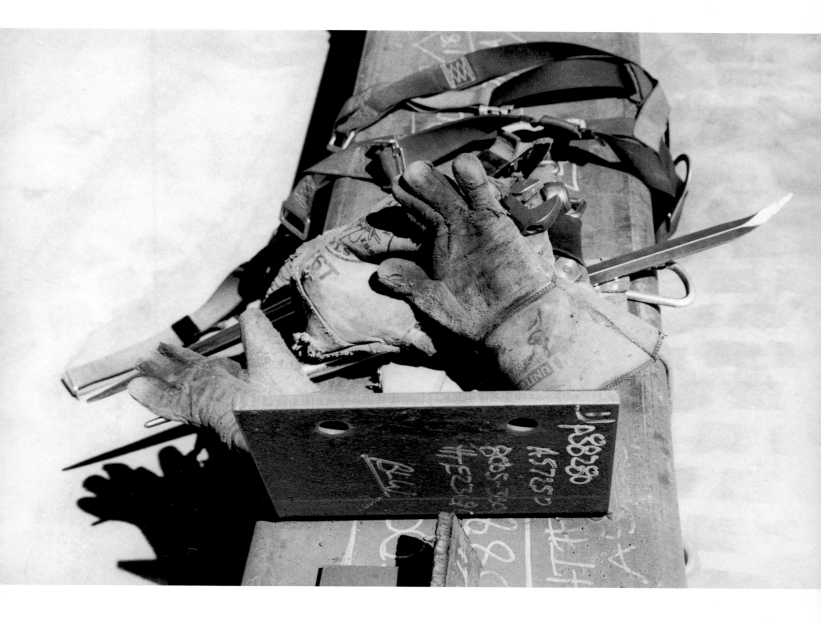

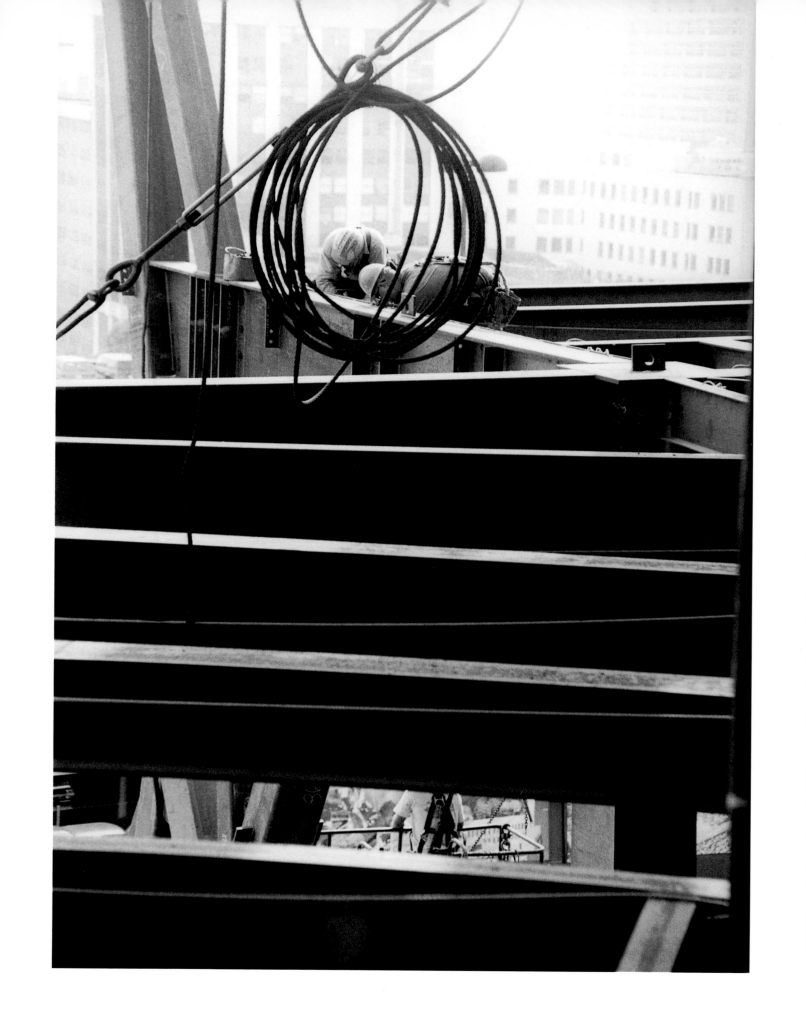

Once a piece of iron has been raised it rarely is sent back to the ground. It is up to the ironworker to make it fit. Piedmont Brown, a connector for 25 years, emphasized this point to me, "Ironworkers can fix nearly anything. Even if the iron fabrication is not done correctly, we will make it fit 99% of the time."

Fear

"Of course I'm afraid of heights, but I turn fear to respect because I know what heights can do to me. That respect grows larger with experience and age. I have a little girl and two young boys. They make it more important I come home safely every night."
—Johnny O'Kane

Even with the help of a crane and other modern tools, raw strength, courage, and daring are attributes every ironworker must possess

"You have to be physically prepared and make sure you are not going to get hit by the iron. When a forty-foot header comes toward you it usually rests on two beams before you work with it. The danger is that the two chokers can create slack when the header is on the beams and come right at you when you don't expect it."

−Joe Connery, 23, ironworker 2 1/2 years

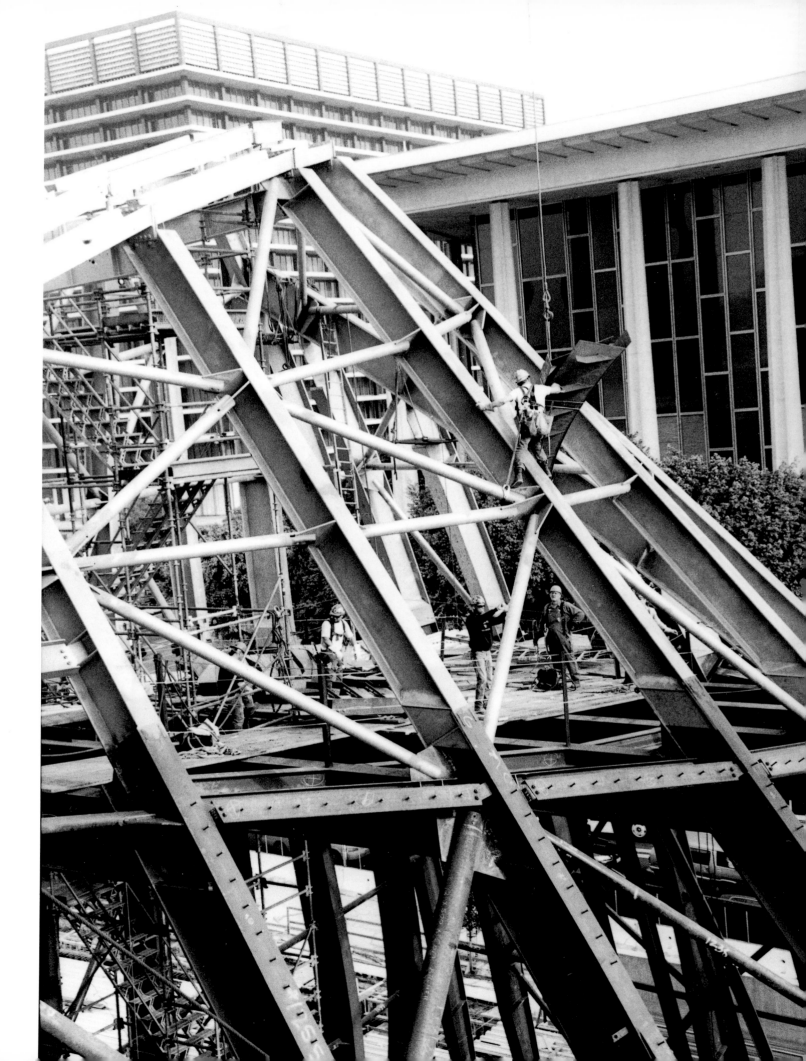

Floors

"Rodbusters" are the ironworkers who carry, place, and tie off the reinforcing bars in preparation for the concrete pouring that will immediately follow completion of their work.

Placing the metal decking over the iron
beams is also a job ironworkers are called
to perform. It, too, is dangerous, back-
breaking, hard work. "Deckers" leave their
own geometric art both in the preparation
of their work and in their finished product.

"I love it out here with the guys. In an office
there are too many women running around. I can
see what I've done and I can be proud. This job
has really asked a lot of us. Nothing is straight,
nothing is square, everything is cut to fit."
—Jim Noson, ironworker 16 years, rodbuster

"The most difficult part of the job is the physical demands—always bending over or carrying the rebar. It's tough on your back, knees and ankles. After 20-30 years of this you'll pay for it. On the way home your legs will cramp up, your back hurts, but the next day you wake up and you can't wait to get to work."
—Jim Noson, ironworker 16 years

Epilogue

"Gil has a good rapport with the ironworkers. That is not an easy thing to do. We're
not the friendliest people around."
—Mitch Shanholtzer, ironworker 21 years,
3rd generation.

Gil is at right in dark jacket.

The traditional "topping out" involves hoist-
ing the last beam signed by the workers to
the top of the structure where an ever-
green tree will perch for the next few days.

Photographer's Statement

It was early summer 2001. Looking up, I was driving by the construction site of the Walt Disney Concert Hall. I did a double take. I couldn't quite believe what I saw. Yes, I thought to myself, there actually is a man crawling on his hands and knees on a very high arched beam a hundred feet above the ground. I pulled my car over to the curb and reached into my briefcase for my always-present camera. It wasn't there.

The next day I returned fully prepared with two cameras, three lenses, and plenty of black and white film. I set up behind the Los Angeles Music Center across the street. I saw the same man who had been crawling on the beam the previous day being hoisted up near the top of the structure. I began taking photographs. He got out of the hoist and climbed a beam where he promptly began to tighten a bolt. He moved to another beam. He balanced himself precariously with one foot on a three-inch steel flange and the other foot on a small steel step. Holding onto the beam with one hand he inserted what looked like a one and one-half foot long tapered steel tool through some holes joining two beams. The tool did not go in very far. He took out a heavy sledgehammer, brought it behind his back and then swung it. A second or two later I heard a metal whacking sound that seemed to reverberate through the entire structure. He hit the tool three or four times before he was able to insert a

large bolt and nut. I thought if I were swinging that sledgehammer even once from where the worker was positioned, I would be dead. I wouldn't have had the physical strength to swing it with one hand and still maintain my balance.

For the next hour, I continued to photograph. I was fascinated by the geometry of the architecture and the daredevil ironworkers. Most were balanced perilously on steel beams, platforms, and cranes more than a hundred feet off the ground. But these men were not simply workers. They were legendary – they were ironworkers.

Darrell Cowles, the man I had originally seen crawling on a beam, is one of those ironworkers. He is a friendly, handsome, 36-year-old husband and father of a young girl. He works as a "connector" in the "raising gang." His description makes it sound easy: "My partner and I are the first ones to touch the steel as the crane lowers it into place, and it is our job to connect the steel member to another steel member." Every time I saw Darrell or his partner, Craig Castor, they were 80 to 120 feet off the ground, either working the steel member into place or trying to get the boltholes aligned. Although the workers wore safety straps, anyone could see that this was extremely demanding and dangerous work. A few days later I went to a darkroom and printed some of the images I had shot. I liked what I saw.

Jack Holt is the Secretary-Treasurer of Ironworkers Union Local 433. He answered my telephone call not with a "hello" but with, "Hi Gil, we'll send you a thousand dollars." When I told him I was not running for political office and that I was interested in photographing his ironworkers, he invited me to the construction site.

At the request of the union, I took a group photograph of the 130 ironworkers – 129 men and 1 woman – at the site. I then began to take individual and partner photographs of the ironworkers, and architectural photographs of the building. When I printed a photograph of an ironworker who could be identified, I would give him an 8"x10" print. I was on the construction site several hours a week over an initial period of about three months. I wanted others to feel the awe I felt watching these workers. In late summer, I began to think my work might lend itself to a book. The Los Angeles Philharmonic staff recommended that I contact Balcony Press about publishing.

I knew that when the building was completed in October 2003, its architect, Frank Gehry, and his partners, would receive much deserved credit for designing such a stunning and successful concert hall. But I also knew that the ironworkers, who made Frank Gehry's concept a reality, would be forgotten. When the first concertgoers enter the hall, they will not see the bones, veins, muscle, and tissue that make up this building. They will

not appreciate that the swooping, curved and angled walls, columns, skylights, and ceiling panels are there because, somehow, ironworkers were able to hang, bolt, and weld the steel that made this possible. They will not realize that each of the 12,500 pieces of primary steel, ranging in size from 13 inches to 110 feet, and weighing up to 165,000 pounds, is unique and individually created, shaped or angled for its respective architectural or structural purpose.

Whenever I was at the construction site, I would notice the number of people on the street looking at the building with awe, disbelief, admiration, and occasionally, dismissal. I talked with some of these people and invariably they would ask about the "wonderful," "far out," "extreme," "crazy," or "indecipherable" architecture. But they would also marvel about the ironworkers. "They're incredible!" "How do they do it?" "What they're doing is impossible!" "They're crazy. Someone is going to get killed." Ironworkers are passionate about their jobs and their union. As ironworkers, they believe they are special. Greg Knutson, the general contractor's project superintendent agrees: "They have earned the pride they display. They are always the first ones on the project. They have the most dangerous jobs and they have done great work." My respect for ironworkers increased when I learned about the role many of them were playing in the aftermath of 9-11. From all over the nation, ironworkers left their jobs to volunteer with the rescue efforts in New York City.

Contrary to their image, ironworkers are not just hulks. An apprentice ironworker must complete three years of community college level training to become a Journeyman Ironworker. For three years, the apprentice must attend school three hours a night, three nights a week, after he has finished his normal work shift. Apprentices are taught the basics of ironwork: structural steel, rebar, rigging, and welding. Having attended some of their classes and reviewed their workbooks, I was particularly impressed with the consistent emphasis on safety and teamwork. The apprentices are taught that everything they do is part of a collaborative effort. Ironworker brothers and sisters are expected to watch out for one another and no one works alone. Ironwork is our nation's third most dangerous occupation. Amazingly, no one has been killed on this job site.

As this book goes to press, the geometric shapes and contours of the hung steel still create visual magic especially in the light and shadows of early morning and late afternoon. The ironworker, balancing himself high above the ground, constantly fighting gravity and the thirty to sixty pounds of tools and equipment he must carry, is no longer there. He is gone. He is working on another project.

For thirty-two years I was a member of the Los Angeles County District Attorney's Office. During those thirty-two years, beginning with the birth of my daughter, I have been an active photographer. Urban photography has been my passion. This project relates to that discipline, but it also combines three other passions of mine: people, music, and architecture.

The Walt Disney Concert Hall will be a feast for your eyes, ears, and spirits. Whether or not you are one of the lucky people who will attend a performance, I hope this book will give you a deeper appreciation for this building. It is the result of the collaborative efforts of various individuals who have great dreams, commitment, stamina, and professional abilities. It started with the Los Angeles County Board of Supervisors and the Music Center's Board of Trustees. Then, from the architects to the general contractor, structural engineers, mechanical engineers, electrical engineers, acoustical consultants, theater consultants, landscape architects, and ultimately to the trades people who actually put the building together as you see it, these are the men and women who made this building possible. Perhaps these images will increase the awe and respect you have not just for the building, but also for the people who built it. If so, then this photographic project will indeed have been successful.

—GIL GARCETTI

Ironworkers

HERRICK

Ara Agahayans
Russel Ahlgrim
Nefty Aldana
Joe Allen
Hector Alvarado
Richard Alvarez
John Barbor
Alex Barbosa
Doug Bratschi
Donald Breceno
Peadmont Brown
Brandon Buffington
Migel Calderon
John Cangey
Lucian Carlier
Bobby Casso
Craig Caster
Darrel Clowes
Jack Colin
Joe Connery
Leo Corronza
Raul Cuevas
Floyd Dalton
Mark Day
Mark Dehlery
William Deyling
Sal Diaz
Sue Egberts
Mike Elwell
Dan Estep
Oscar Fiero
Barry Fike
Edgar Flores
Fred Garza
Javier Gonzales
Jesse Gonzales
Albert Gomez
Sean Grief
Jose Grijalva
Lance Harris
Abel Herrera
Phillip Holt
Phil Hosier
James Imbot
Scott Jackson
Jeff Johnson
Carl Kaddour
John Reily
William Rogers
Richard Roth

Troy Lavander
Chris Maher
Joe Marrings
Carmello Martinez
Mike McCabe
Danny Martinez Jr.
Danny Martinez Sr.
Brent May
Duane Matthews
Paul McDaid
Clinton Michael
C.W. Neves
Shane O'Brien
John O'Conner
Johnny O'Kane
Paul Pearse
Ernie Penuelas
Tommy Pico Jr.
Alex Piementel
Fred Powell
Sal Ramirez
Vince Ramos
Frank Reinmiller
Henry Rivas
Luis Rivas
Henry Roa
William Rogers
Charles Ruggles
Jose Sanchez
Mark Seymour
Tom Shanks
Art Tabuchi
Jeremiah Thomas
Effren Tinoco
Russell Toll
Hecter Villapando
Frank Walker
David Warren
Rolondo Waters
Paul Watkins
Bob Williams

PERMASTEELISA

Fernando Acuna
Steve Andelich
William Anderson
Edgar Apodaca
Cesar Avilez
Gary Bailey
John Cangey
Shelby Scott Cline
Tim Crail
Richard Diaz
Susan Egberts
Steve Enriquez
Kevin Frizelle
George Fuller
Rodrigo Gallegos
Melton Gaston
James Graham
Tom Grillo
Steve Geer
Dave Golightly
Tom Golightly
Paul Gravett
Mike Harris
Thurman Hornbucks III
David Kennamer
Edward Knaus
Jose Mayorga
Ramiro Mayorga
Steve Magles
Juan Miqueo
Arend Oudyk
Rick Peterson
Alan Pinley
John Pridemore Jr.
Richard Robinson
Kevin Shanholtzer
Mitchell Shanholtzer
Michael Silvey
Ron Smith
Richard Van Wagenen
Filipe Villareal
Gabriel Villareal
Jose Villarreal
Oscar Villareal
Ryan Walton
Tom Weemhof
Bob Williams

EAGLE IRON

Tom Barnett
Mark Hale
Dennis Hattersley
Lennie Mc Neal
Robert Pendley
Richard Rijos
Jose Rodriguez
Sean Seems
Don Taylor
James Arvizu
Melvin Banegas
Mark Bell
Henry Besida
James Boehm
James Campbell
Dennis Chandler
Frank Folkes
William Garrett
Miguel Gonzalez
Chris Hammond
Abel Herrera
Michael Hoss
Miguel Huizer
Randy King
Juan Lopez
Gregorio Martinez
Jeff Mason
Jehn Morris
Cruz Ortega
Lou Penna
Salamon Perez
Salvador Perez
Kevin Pevoteaux
Deaudrey Pryor
Derick Shannon
Frazer Slessor
Art Truex
Nick Twenhaufel
Michael Wood
Arnold Yackley Jr.

BICKERTON

Mark Allen
Rene Bernal
David Canas
Stevie Christal
Ian Colman
Lauren Davis
Alfred Lopez
Tracy Miller
Clinton Murray
Edward Paulsen
Jonathan Rijos

Acknowledgments

I did not begin this photographic project with the idea of publishing a book. As I shared my photographs of the ironworkers and the building with the ironworkers and their families they seemed to experience recognition of their efforts never before imagined from the outside world. Many ironworkers and their family members encouraged me to turn my photographic project of them and the building into a book. To them I owe my first thanks. My proceeds from the sale of this book are going to the Ironworkers International Scholarship Fund. As much as I enjoy sensing the pride that ironworkers carry regarding their work, I can just imagine the immense pride that an ironworker would have seeing a son or daughter graduate from college on an ironworker scholarship.

My special thanks for making this book possible go to several individuals and companies. Jack Holt, Secretary-Treasurer, Ironworkers Local 433, arranged unlimited access to the work site. Herrick and Mortenson companies permitted me on the site during all hours. Frank Gehry, his partners and associates, early on agreed to help me with my book. They were both generous with their time and instructive in teaching me enough about creating the Walt Disney Concert Hall which helped me with the images I was photographing. My editor, Jennifer Volland, gave me the moral support, as well as the editorial help that every photographer-writer needs. Thanks, too, to Navigator Press and Peter Shamray for the patience and expertise in scanning the photographs for best possible reproduction. My book designer, Kurt Hauser, deserves thanks not only for the superb book design and layout, but also for meeting the formidable deadlines in getting the book to the printer. My final acknowledgement goes to Ann Gray, my publisher. She is indeed a professional who very calmly and knowledgably guided me through my first publishing process. She has also been willing to gamble that an ex-Los Angeles County District Attorney can create a successful photographic book project. I hope she is right. To her and the many other people not mentioned on this page, I thank you.

Publisher's Note

Over the many years we have been publishing art and architecture books I am constantly amazed at the passion our authors bring to their work. They work extraordinary hours getting the perfect photograph, crafting the right sentence, and confirming facts. This book has brought home yet again my appreciation of their efforts. Gil Garcetti, in creating this book, has literally donned the welder's mask and come as close to becoming an ironworker as an attorney can get. He has ridden hoists, strapped on the safety, taken apprenticeship classes, welded steel, and spent hundreds of hours interviewing individuals involved in the design and construction of the building from patrons to broom pushers. He has taken an estimated 1800 photographs.

Gil has delved into far-flung topics such as Frank Gehry's sources of inspiration, the logic of the CATIA computer system, the kind of gloves the workers use, and what their favorite jobsite foods are. The reason I offer this note is that 99% of the fascinating things he has learned will not be obviously apparent in this book and they are probably better left out. Nevertheless, they inform his photographs and his text in a profound and subtle way that the reader is sure to appreciate.

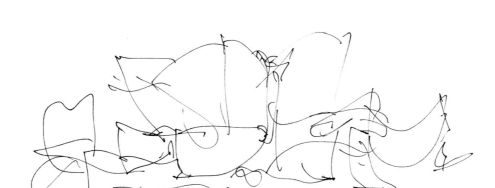

EXOV-GMAND   DISNEY HALL

Frank Gehry's concept sketch.

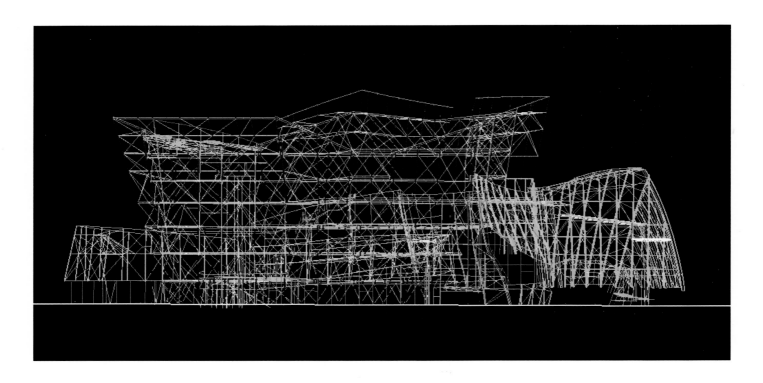

Computer model of steel framing.

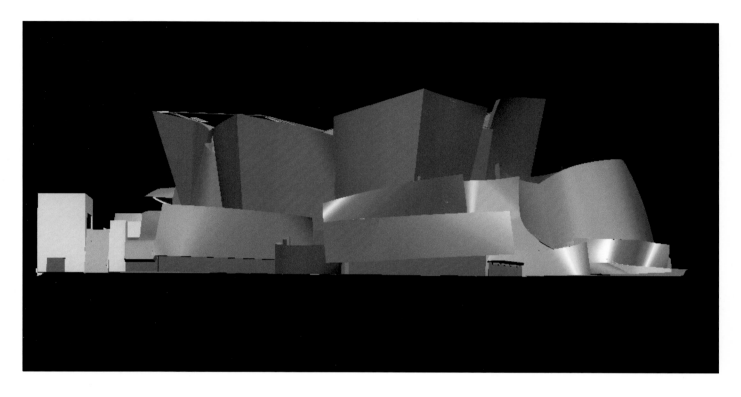

Finished building model.

Published in the United States of
America by Balcony Press 2002
Design by Kurt Hauser
Printed by Navigator Press,
Monrovia, California

These photographs were taken with a
Nikon F100 using Kodak Tri-X film and
printed on Ilford multi-grade fiber paper.

LCCN: 2002103812
ISBN 1-890449-15-6